Tomorrow's Global Leaders Today

Executive Reflection: Working Wisely in Turbulent Times

JACKIE ARNOLD and ELAINE PATTERSON

This book is dedicated to leaders everywhere who give of themselves to make the world a better place.

Leading needs to be seen as a vocation – as a deep honour and a bestowed privilege – to co-create teams, organizations, communities and systems, which sustainably and generatively attend to the wellbeing of all.

We want to extend our heartfelt thanks and deepest appreciation for all the leaders and people practitioners we have had the pleasure to meet, work and talk with. You have all – in your own ways – inspired our thinking and ignited our desire to creatively resource leaders. We hope this book will help you to lean into – and effectively address – today's herculean demands for change and transformation with curiosity, compassion, courage and wisdom for the wellbeing of all and health of our planet.

Jackie Arnold and Elaine Patterson

Praise for
Tomorrow's Global Leaders Today
Executive Reflection: Working Wisely in Turbulent Times

Many global leaders are probably aware of the UN Global Goals for 2030, but I wonder how many are taking a critical look at their leadership styles and approaches that will equip them to create and build sustainable organizations. In this new e-book from Jackie Arnold and Elaine Patterson, we have a fresh, research-based, energising approach to leadership that supports leaders to behave, think and develop in ways that will enable them to lead more effectively in the relentlessly turbulent world in which we are now living. This text not only offers a philosophical challenge to leaders but also provides practical suggestions and ideas to guide leaders to change their approaches.

Through engaging in the techniques and methods of Executive Reflection, the authors offer leaders a distinct leadership approach and process that invites them to pause, take stock, be still and reflect, as integral leadership practices. Rather than allowing the turbulence of today's world to buffet and churn them around, here Executive Reflection provides leaders with inspiration, maps and resources so that they can choose how to act rather than being tossed from one reactive decision to another. Through engaging in Executive Reflection, leaders can create some containment for their own way of being and at the same time, create some sense of stability for their teams and organizations.

Dr. Alison Hodge from Alison Hodge Associates Ltd.
EMCC EIA Accredited Master Coach & EMCC ESIA Accredited Coaching Supervisor;
Consultant to Faculty and Curriculum with Coaching Supervision Academy;
Chair of Governor Members for EMCC

This, the first in a series, offers a new take on leadership style by featuring evidence-based research as underpinning the value and impact of reflective practice. You're shown how to continuously evolve yourself and others in ways that conjoin working practices today and what to anticipate for the future.

Executive Reflection recognizes demands beyond VUCA through the influences of diversity and working both virtually and globally. The text refreshingly recognizes that 'busyness' does not always achieve sustainable results. Fresh thinking is gained through giving reflective practice a 'new twist'.

Today's leaders have to encourage engagement and vigilance in avoiding the disruption of negative subcultures. The superficiality of generalisms that fuel stereotyping others is replaced by generating interest in the deeper complexities of each individual. Diversity is fertile territory for expanding the performance of our people resource. We're invited to reflect on and accept personal biases that lead to misinterpretations and to talk about issues! The message is be brave in conversation. This is not a big ask; it's an essential ask for the leadership of tomorrow.

Case studies from the authors' personal experience illustrate challenges from cross-cultural working. A range of practices guide you into Executive Reflection that brings your uniqueness into leadership practices. No more glossing over passing thoughts about how you might have done things differently, or not even noticing when doing something different would have achieved a more positive outcome. The bigger goal of the series is to support leaders in having the personal expertise to meet the UN Global Goals for 2030.

Dr. Lise Lewis
EMCC International Special Ambassador
Ch.FCIPD; MBA; EMCC EIA Accredited Master Coach Mentor; EMCC ESIA Accredited Coach Mentor Supervisor; Bluesky International; Provider of EMCC EQA Coach Mentor and ESQA Coach Supervisor Training

A timely and opportune, highly valuable contribution to the acute and chronic challenges of leadership, both now and tomorrow. Jackie and Elaine take the latest neuro research and blend this with the tried and tested techniques of reflective practice to create an entirely new approach to leadership, fit for the post-modern world. The researchers have listened hard to the woes of global leaders and created a set of pragmatic tools, customized for, and adaptable to, an environment of systemic, unrelenting change and ambiguity. Accessible for all, I look forward to seeing Executive Reflection on the daily agenda of all managers and leaders, at every level of every organisation.

Carol McLachlan
MA FCA BFP, Chartered Accountant and Executive Business Coach, ICAEW Council Member, currently researching boundaryless careers in the digital, virtual world of AI for PhD

This book is so timely in this world of dynamic evolving change that we find ourselves in. The way the authors have captured the importance and vital role that reflection plays in executives' lives is well written with some outstanding research. The power and impact of spending time in reflection is highlighted and amplified. The book clearly explains that new ways of leading are needed and they are needed right now. This is a must read, you can't help but reflect yourself whilst reading it.

Mandy Flint
CEO, Senior Leader and Advisor; Leadership and Cultural Change Strategist, and Amazon bestselling, multi award winning Author, *The Leader's Guide to Impact*

Having the opportunity to participate in this project has revealed such an exciting application of supervision approaches, tools and creative reflective options. It has been extraordinary to see how significant and impactful these wider conversations have been. Leaders can only benefit from the invitation to engage their people in rich, diverse and quite unique ways that meet the critical issues at the threshold of the VUCA GVD interface.

Karyn Prentice
International Executive Coach, Coaching Supervisor, Teacher, Writer and Reflective Thinking Partner

I have worked with Jackie as a personal coach on and off for the past eighteen years and I have found that her easy to understand concepts and her communication is clear and very effective. The use of Clean Language for example, has been helpful for me as an Englishman leading multinational organizations and has also been invaluable as it helped me build strong leadership teams throughout my career. I use Jackie's concepts in my day-to-day coaching with my multinational team, which has helped them develop their leadership capabilities. Finally, it is good to see that coaching is being recognized as a key tool for all leaders and managers globally.

Ian Dawkin
CEO ITC Global, Head of Global Network OperationPanasonic Avionics

Working with Elaine has been a transformational experience, in my growth as a human being as well as professionally. She helped me breakthrough some deeply rooted obstacles, by first seeing them through creative and reflective lenses. Elaine challenged me in ways I didn't realise I needed and on things I didn't know were there. Highly recommend Elaine's practices, perspectives, and supervision.

Raoul Encinas
Founder PhosLabs

Foreword

There is so much turbulence in today's busy business world. Today's and tomorrow's successful leaders have to simultaneously navigate stormy seas while delivering the numbers, retaining talent, stimulating innovation, cultivating agile cultures and future-proofing their organizations. One global CEO I recently interviewed (as part of Henley Business School's Tomorrow's Leaders Today's Leadership Development study) shared the impactful metaphor of having to retrofit a plane in mid-flight while flying into increasing turbulence, keeping the ground-crew up-to-date and all the inflight crew happy! Welcome to what Jackie Arnold and Elaine Patterson call the VUCA GVD world.

We are in the midst of a metamorphosis that affects our way of leading at deep and partly unconscious levels, transforming how and why we do things and the purpose and meaning we bring to our organizations. Executive Reflection – the flow of Retreat, Reflect and Return – is at the heart of this metamorphosis: an emerging 'way of being' in our leadership consciousness that up-stretches us to the next-stage of leading life-affirming organizations fit for the future.

In this practical and easy-to-digest guide, the co-authors explore the importance of Executive Reflection for the new-norm of leadership now demanded by the VUCA GVD world. This exciting yet volatile world of ours is steeped in relationality. To relate wisely amid this ever-changing relationality, we need to still ourselves which, amid the busyness of business, is an art. It is this artfulness that the co-authors clarify for us. It is the stillness within us where the new-norm spawns. It's the stillness within that allows the eye of the heart to see rightly amid stormy seas.

Giles Hutchins

Chair of The Future Fit Leadership Academy, Founder of Leadership Immersions, Co-Founder of Regenerators and Author

Copyright

Published and Produced 2020 by IngramSpark

Cover and text design: meadencreative.com

Editor: Emma Dickens

ISBN: 978-1-9164560-7-5 Tomorrow's Global Leaders Today Print Version

© Jackie Arnold and Elaine Patterson, 2020

The moral right of the author has been asserted. All rights reserved. Without limiting the rights under copyright reserved above, no part of this publication may be produced, stored in or introduced into a retrieval system, or transmitted in any form or by any means (electronic, mechanical, photocopying, recording or otherwise) without the prior written permission of both the copyright owner and the above publisher of this book.

All proceeds will be gifted to help support the achievement of the 2030 United Nations Global Goal No. 4 for Sustainable Development. Global Goal No. 4 is the goal for Quality Education which is aiming to ensure inclusive and equitable quality education and promote lifelong opportunities for all by 2030. Please see www.globalgoals.org for more information.

Contents

Introduction	The Bigger Picture	10
Chapter 1	Executive Reflection: *A New and Distinct Leadership Style*	16
Chapter 2	Our VUCA GVD World: *The Perfect Storm*	20
Chapter 3	Executive Reflection: *The Port in the Perfect Storm*	34
Chapter 4	Executive Reflection: *Orienteering and Navigation*	48
Call to Action		56
More Background to the Project		59
References		61

Glossary

GVD: GVD was coined by the authors and is an acronym for Global, Virtual and Diverse environments

VUCA: VUCA was coined by Johannson and is an acronym for Volatile, Uncertain, Complex and Ambiguous environments[1]

INTRODUCTION
The Bigger Picture

> *In times of turmoil the danger lies not in the turmoil but in facing it with yesterday's logic.*
>
> Peter Drucker[1]

Wherever we find ourselves living and working, we are all in a time of radical uncertainty and unprecedented change on a global scale. The internet has exposed us to new challenges and opportunities and has made leadership more complex, more nuanced, more stressful and more exposing. Yesterday's ways and logic are no longer enough as the winds of fundamental social, economic, ecological and political change buffet us. New and different ways of thinking, relating, learning and leading are required for co-creating tomorrow's futures today. 'Problems,' as Albert Einstein said, 'cannot be solved from the consciousness which created them.'[2]

Otto Scharmer encapsulated the extent of today's ecological, social, spiritual and leadership crisis with the following statistics:[3]

- Our world economies consume the resources of 1.5 planets. Our current consumption is outstripping the resources of earth to support us.
- The world's eight richest individuals have as much wealth as the 3.6bn people who make up the poorest half of the world.
- 800,000 people commit suicide each year – a number greater than those killed annually by war, murder and natural disaster put together.

In addition, as Lois Bushong has observed:[4]

> No generation before now has had so many of its members simultaneously living in, between and among countless cultural worlds as today.

In September 2015 world leaders at an historic United Nations Summit adopted the 2030 United Nations Agenda for Sustainable Development. The seventeen Sustainable Development Goals came into forced on the 1st January 2016, all countries will mobilize to end all forms of poverty, fight inequalities and tackle climate change, while ensuring the no one is left behind.[5] The bar is set. How then can leaders in their different role, organizations and locations help to achieve these goals?

In a recent survey it was found that:[6]

- 84% of businesses surveyed did not currently have a global strategy in place for training future leaders.
- 92% of respondents said that critical thinking and 86% said that judgement and decision-making were the most important qualities that a leader needed.

This is where Executive Reflection comes in.

About the Authors

We are both International Executive Coaches and Coaching Supervisors. Jackie's company – Coach4Executives – specializes in cross-cultural and intercultural leadership, communication and training. Elaine's company – The Centre for Reflection and Creativity – specializes in reflection, creativity and people development.

In 2015, our story of working together began when we were introduced to each other by Edna Murdoch from the Coaching Supervision Academy Ltd. (CSA). Edna brought us together because she knew of our shared passion for fresh thinking in leadership discourse. Up until then we had been exploring separately how to better shape the way global leaders lead and wanted to reshape the current discourse concerned as the 2010 IBM Global CEO Study had so succinctly stated that:[7]

> *The great majority of CEOs expect that business complexity is going to increase and … more than half doubt their ability to manage it. The sheer difficulty of keeping a corporation afloat in such turbulent economic, political, and social water is beyond most leaders' experience and capacity.*

About the Tomorrow's Global Leaders Today Series

In this, the first of our series, we present Executive Reflection as a new international leadership style and antidote to global leadership challenges, wherever you are and whomever you lead.

Executive Reflection can offer the inspiration, maps, support and resources leaders need to navigate today's radical uncertainty. It enables them to captain new futures for themselves and their teams and organizations and encourages them to help implement the UN's 2030 Global Goals.

This book will explore the What, Why and How of Executive Reflection. Book 2 in the series will explore the realities of cross-cultural global working and Book 3 will explore the 1:1 practice, training and CPD necessary for coaches, supervisors and organizational development (OD) professionals to become 1:1 Executive Reflection Practitioners.

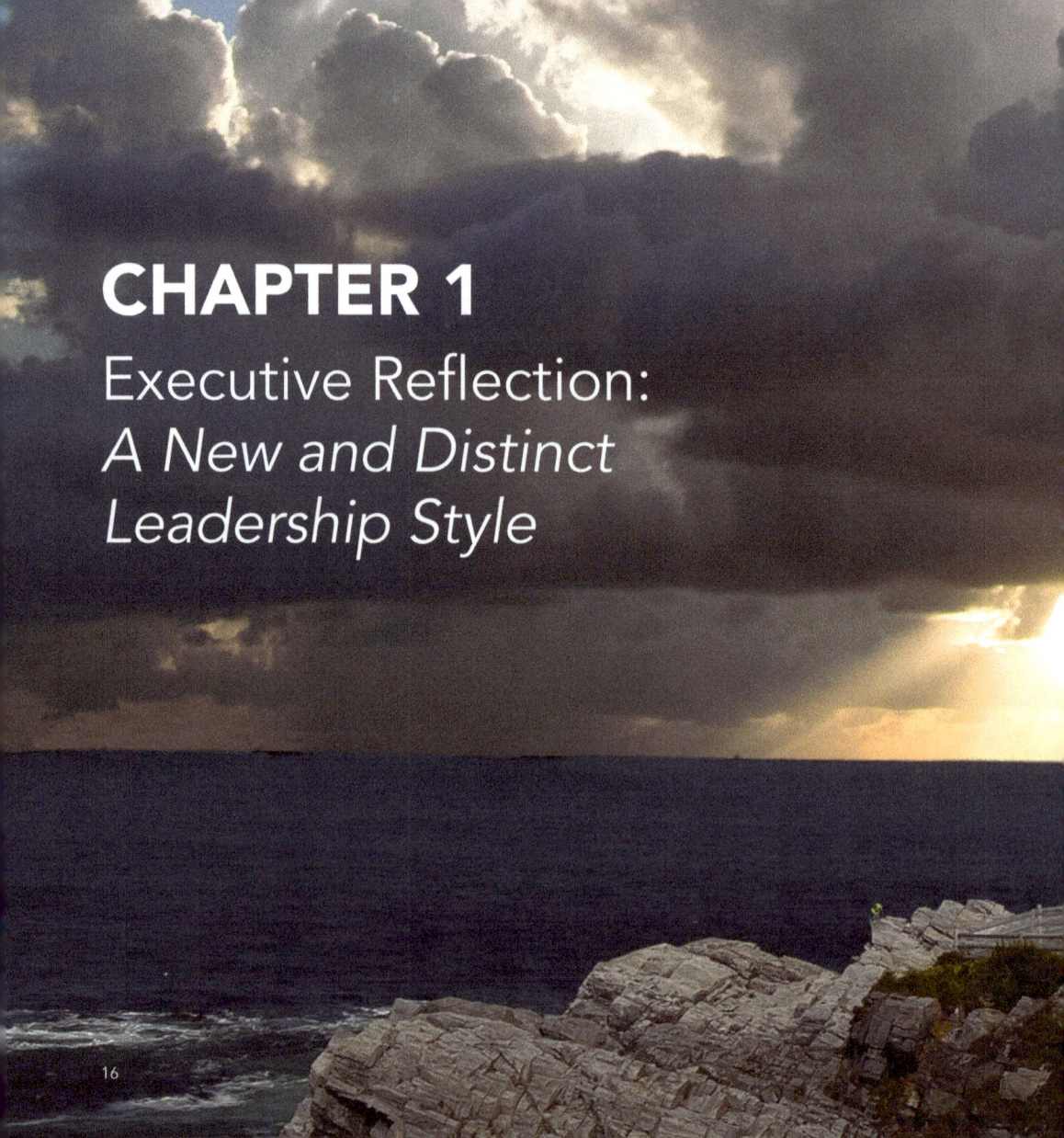

CHAPTER 1
Executive Reflection:
*A New and Distinct
Leadership Style*

History teaches us what happens when we fail to respond to what is new and different to us; when we fail to learn, adapt and evolve; and when we sleepwalk into the future. We are shown the price of failing to do these things by upheavals such as the banking crisis, Brexit and climate change, as well as by noticing our social and spiritual inertia, and observing the rise and fall of politicians and business leaders. New and different thinking is needed.

Executive Reflection complements all that you already know. It also elevates your leadership, enabling you to work with the unknown: to be the lighthouse; to value inquiry, curiosity and courage as the bridges to recognizing what wants to emerge.

We have therefore defined Executive Reflection as:

> A distinct leadership style which enables global leaders to lean into today's VUCA GVD world and through a range of powerful reflective processes discover how to wisely adapt, evolve, and transform not only themselves but also their teams and their organizations to both navigate the present and co-create new futures for the good of all.

Executive Reflection gives us a way to navigate ourselves in our work both from the inside out and from the outside in. As Hilary Owen explains:[1]

> People cannot be molded to be the same. Becoming a leader is an individual process and fundamental to the process is 'learning'. However, the learning is not through 'training' alone, but through personal experience and learning from that experience. When learning from experience occurs, it involves looking inwards at who we are. It means a deep awareness of who we are and the sort of human being we want to become. Once we know this, it can be expressed in our relationships and actions at work.

Executive Reflection works because it brings a range of powerful reflective processes to the fore. These are explored in Chapter 4. Often in the general busyness of business and the urgency for quick fixes in our VUCA GVD world – which is explored in further detail in Chapter 2 – we can rush from one quick-fire solution to another. We can forget to push the pause button: to reflect and to wonder if there might be another way; to notice the inconvenient truth; to work out our blind spots or to appreciate the larger trends or patterns at work. We also risk losing ourselves as we work – and forgetting that leadership does not exist in a vacuum but in the relationships we build across and between people, generations, cultures and continents in order to get the work done. We can forget that WHO we are and WHO we are becoming is HOW we work – and that this directly determines the impact we have and the results we get.[2]

This has four serious implications for the quality of our leadership:

1. Neuroscience research teaches us that when we are hyper busy we shut down our executive functioning and our ability to be creative.[3] We also shut down access to our other intelligences: to the knowing in our heart, body and soul which are needed – in ourselves and in the people in our teams – for making wise choices and decisions.[4]

2. Hyper busyness means that we can fail to make the time to mindfully nurture key relationships, which in turn can lead to multiple miscuing, misunderstandings and disengagement.

3. Reflection is often missed or skipped over in the rush to be seen to be doing or taking some or any action.[5]

4. Reflection is the gateway to new thinking, creativity and innovation.[6] Major benefits for both the individual and the team or organization are lost when time and processes for reflection are not created. The costs of not reflecting are loss of understanding, loss of creativity, loss of relationships, poor decision-making, loss of energy and loss of productivity.[7]

Figure 1: Value of Reflecting

Figure 2: Costs of Not Reflecting

Executive Reflection can help to centre and ground us. It can help us see our next steps and the horizon we are heading towards clearly. It can keep us flexible enough to change course or direction as the weather changes.

CHAPTER 2
Our VUCA GVD World: *The Perfect Storm*

New ways of leading – seeing, thinking, relating, behaving and creating, at both the deeply personal and collective levels – are therefore now mission critical, not only for individuals but for organizations to create a secure future and build vital international relationships in our global, virtual and diverse (GVD) world. The acronym GVD was created to capture the essence of business and organizational life today.

GVD is defined as follows:

- Global – the global marketplace, the worldwide nature, stretch and web of work which can cross continents, time zones, cultures and language.
- Virtual – computers, the web and digital technology have enabled leaders to reach, communicate, co-ordinate and deliver work to customers and clients globally.
- Diverse – the cultural mix and blending of many different countries, languages, identities, cultures, races and languages which can exist in just one person, in a team and in an organization.

We believe leaders now need to alter course as they shape vision, goals and deliverables, and inspire performance. They need to understand why employees are disengaged, demotivated and largely reactive. They should grasp the power of grounding and presence instead of operating merely from the intellect. Understanding is also required to release hidden potential and creativity.

In short, leaders need to take time for reflective practice which gives leaders the power to choose their direction and ways of working rather than it choosing them. Consequently they will have greater global influence.

Understanding GVD

Global

As business leaders working in a more remotely controlled, global and multicultural environment, it is vitally important to consider the effect of our own cultural influences on the dealings we have with others. It is necessary to reflect on and voice possible assumptions, cultural biases and misconceptions early on.

This is because we have all been brought up in different environments with vastly different cultural influencers. We also have diverse filters and even two people in the same family can differ greatly in how they react and express their beliefs. Every society has cultural values which influence how individuals think and behave: ideas about what is right or wrong, what is fair or unfair, what is honest or dishonest. We cannot stereotype but broadly cultural values can assist us in our understanding of cross-cultural relationships and help to guide us when doing business internationally.

The authors, who have lived abroad and work internationally, have realized we need to learn more about unconscious bias and cultural norms and to adapt accordingly. This is in order to build and maintain strong lasting productive relationships while doing business globally. We need to avoid stereotyping and generalizations. We need to become curious about how each person's own story and life experiences shape their own culture and how they fit into their wider cultural context. This includes their communities, how they live, and the organizations in which they work. When working cross-culturally, we need to take into consideration all the wider cultural aspects of an individual's story – not only those which are visible, but also those which are hidden. This means leaders and team members need to be open and curious about WHO each person is so that they can understand HOW they think, relate, learn and work, in order to get the best from each other. These include what has made – and makes – an individual's assumptions, manner, mindset, values, beliefs, rituals, religion, laws (written and unwritten), innovation, customs, ceremonies, social institutions, myths and legends, attitudes, and accepted/not-accepted behaviours, and their needs for safety and trust. Sensitivity to these diverse societal, cultural and individual filters, differences and values is key to working cross-culturally and can help to guide us when doing business internationally.

Figure 1: Understanding Each Person's Lived Experience

It is important that leaders find ways to put judgments aside and take the time to prepare for international meetings which promote shared understanding, connection, engagement, responsibility and accountability. Failing to find an open and trusting space – where flexibility, tolerance and creativity are welcomed, and where real insights can emerge – may cause a spiral of miscommunication and mistrust, and potentially a loss of business and professional connections.

This can be compounded and complicated further by remote and/or virtual working. We need to be mindful of the potential confusion and misunderstanding modes of communication such as email, Zoom and Skype present, as well as the opportunities they provide. Not only do leaders need to be able to tune into each person's story and adapt accordingly, but they need to be aware of the nuances of each method of conveying it.

Vignette

In the UK, as a general rule, we are reasonably flexible, forward thinking and open minded when doing business. We tolerate unpredictable situations, and this can cause serious problems when doing business in Japan or Russia where they favour planning and are uncomfortable with unstructured or unpredictable situations. According to research from the Cultural Intelligence Centre 2008, in the UK we have a higher tolerance for ambiguity and risk than, for example, the Swiss. When setting up our business in Switzerland it was apparent that our usual ways of working would not be effective. The Swiss are more outcome orientated and expect very detailed and precise documentation. Authority lines are important and a level of risk aversion is the norm.

In the UK we are often less forthright than our US counterparts and more reticent than our French neighbours. It is useful to reflect on our own cultural background and take into consideration differences of opinion and behaviour when doing business globally.

Vignette

When working in Taiwan and Vietnam in the leadership and development arena, high value is placed on status, task and accomplishment. We were therefore aware of possible areas of conflict. We further understood that as females we would encounter gender bias and that our ideas may not be taken seriously by those in authority. Only after we had used reflective practice, built trust, demonstrated sensitivity and shared knowledge openly and without ego, were we able to win respect.

Case Study

The mission of Airbus in 2005 was to bring all four countries (France, Germany, Spain and UK) together to work as one over the next two years. In addition, there was immense pressure to design, develop, construct and bring to market an innovative and specialist aircraft, namely the A380.

Over the next ten years, by using Executive Coaching and Reflective Practice methods and by introducing a coaching culture across the organization, over seventy leaders were supported to achieve their desired leadership outcomes.

These included:

- Repatriation
- Multi-cultural understanding
- Building strong international teams
- Coping with stress and overwhelm
- Effective delegation & work/life balance
- Time management and forward planning
- Succession planning
- Strategic multi-cultural thinking
- Creating time and space for reflection

The priority for Airbus was to build greater cultural awareness and mutual respect. To achieve this they had to break down unconscious bias, and avoid miscommunication. Further, they had to feel comfortable discussing differences and similarities openly. This helped to build trust and bridge the gaps in both knowledge and understanding. It created an atmosphere of collaboration. As experienced ER practitioners we supported the leaders in their use of respectful language and challenged them to reflect on where they might be making assumptions. They were encouraged to do this by frequently checking understanding through Clean Language, then remaining respectful and aware of possible different language interference, cultural values, beliefs and worldviews.

Jackie Arnold

Virtual

Globally we are closer than ever due to technical and global platforms of communication where leaders may be heading up teams of people they have never met in person. We are now faced with global mass communication where a variety of apps, smartphones and video platforms are replacing face-to-face interactions and conversations.

A few years ago, if you wanted to access information on, say, China's economic growth, you would scan the international pages of a newspaper. Today all you need is a search engine and the information you need is at your fingertips. You can email a stranger, or chat online to a colleague across the world, all in the space of a few minutes. This mass communication has forced companies to rethink how they communicate with their customers. They know they need to pay great attention to how they craft and brand their products, and use effective marketing without causing offence in another part of the world.

Another result of computers, apps, smartphones and TV is that we tend not to pay attention for long periods. There is a lack of time for collaboration, building relationships and noticing what is going on around us. Attention is consistently shifting and our active minds are racing from one task to another on autopilot.

When we engage with people virtually, we are less able to connect at a deeper level and to really understand what is going on for them. However, all is not lost. When using Executive Reflection, we can become conscious of those elements, which enhance this virtual communication. We can learn to be more aware of body language, eye contact, shifts in energy.

In this way we can become more present.

How then do we tap into the silence that quietens us down and enables us to be fully present when communicating virtually?

We believe it is by standing back from the individual's situation and as a result not intruding on their way of being. We can enhance this process by reflecting on and being aware of how we are presenting ourselves on the conference call or video platform: still, relaxed and open. We can pay attention to our gestures and notice how they fit with our words and emotions. It is this quality of attention that shows respect and creates a non-judgmental, positive space for employees/peers to explore and grow in. This enables us to notice and understand the intricate, multi-layered relationships we are forming. In this way we can identify how personality types and behaviours affect standards, performance, wellbeing and core values.

When we show genuine curiosity, pay close attention and are fully present we can support employees/peers to clarify their own understanding of sometimes very demanding situations and contexts. When we consider the often complex issues raised during virtual communication, it is of vital importance to be fully in the moment and not distracted by our own situation or the immediate surroundings.

Case Study

A senior executive who was a German national was working and living in Madrid. He was leading a multicultural team made up of French, Italian and Spanish nationals. He was very task focused and outcome orientated and found it hard at first to integrate and build trust among his team. He asked for feedback on his leadership style and multicultural behaviours. He reflected on those aspects of cultural behaviour that can remain assumed or hidden. These were: voice tone, past business experience, cultural norms and traditions, core values and accepted behaviour. In the Mediterranean countries there is generally a higher value placed on longer term planning and building relationships. This leader struggled with the general chitchat about family and friends at the start of meetings. He was unused to rapport building at the start of his one-to-ones and found it hard to 'let go' of his own cultural norms.

Miscommunication occurs when there's a failure to discuss differences and similarities openly. Doing this will help build trust and bridge the gaps in both knowledge and understanding. It will increase confidence and create an atmosphere of collaboration.

One of the most powerful ways for working cross-culturally is to speak from the heart and to stay truly present and authentic. The multinational leaders and teams we work with are encouraged to use reflective practice and to focus on the positive energy they bring to their interactions. This promotes an understanding of how deep listening, acceptance of differences and speaking from the heart are essential.

Diverse

As humans we generally attract and are attracted to those who have similar viewpoints and perspectives to our own. However, as the world effectively gets smaller and communication more instantaneous and wide reaching, we need to adapt, learn from and accept diversity.

Through various personality profiling and psychometrics such as DISC Profiling, FIRO B, Hogan Personality Inventory and MBTI, we understand that in a high-functioning team having different personalities and skillsets is essential.[1] When considering diversity, we also need to delve deeper into the reasons why individuals act and behave in the way they do. These assessments help us broaden our perspectives and shine a light on those areas of behaviour that may be in conflict with others.

We are of the opinion that it is essential for organizations to have a supportive culture. There needs to be a process whereby individuals can raise concerns without fear of reprisals. Diversity cannot be maintained without relevant and robust processes. Real equality is about equal opportunities, individual rights and being heard. We need to seek out and listen to those who see things differently in order to learn and understand those diverse viewpoints.

Executive Reflection is a way for leaders to take valuable time out and ensure there is adequate openness and inclusivity. It allows us to accept new and innovative ways of working and be open to different opinions and perspectives. The authors have seen firsthand how teams from differing backgrounds and cultures can enrich ideas and can have a direct impact on return on investment and the quality of innovation. Due to an increasingly diverse working environment we all need to be aware of our unconscious bias and stereotyping.

When meeting someone for the first time we cannot make assumptions.

Vignette

Julia is a white female with brown curly hair. She has a British mother. She comes across as a Brit and her English is fluent and natural. However, she was brought up for the first sixteen years in Italy by a very strong and close Italian family. Italian, Spanish and Indian cultures place high value on cooperation and collaboration. There is an emphasis on relationships and family values.

Julia became very frustrated when working in the UK for the first time as she was not used to the reserved and individualistic approach of her Boss. She was uncertain how to approach him and upset at the way she was treated. A greater awareness of what core values and cultural influencers individuals bring to the workplace can greatly ease tension and stress.

Vignette

Leaders need to be more curious and to consider that, for example, the Asian man they see who walks into the room for a meeting may have been born in Hong Kong to a Chinese father, but his family may have travelled extensively. His major cultural influencers, therefore, are from Singapore and USA where he was raised by his Japanese mother. He is also what is known as a Third Culture Adult (TCA) meaning that he spent his formative years in a country other than his parents' birthplace. This can cause problems in later life with these TCAs finding themselves cast adrift, unable to understand where they belong. Try asking a TCA where they are from. This is often an impossible question for them to answer.

Increasingly, many of our employees are TCAs and therefore understanding of and openness to diverse ways of being in the world are essential. Being able to adjust leadership behaviours and adapt styles can be the key factor in whether teams work effectively, deals are sealed, and international projects are completed.

To deliver on agreed purposes and agendas, leaders need to be aware of their own cultural makeup and those of each team member to respectfully navigate differences and similarities in:

- Language
- Education
- Upbringing
- Sexual orientation
- Stereotypes
- Media and grapevine
- Voice tone, pace and stress patterns
- Meaning gestures & interpretation
- Cultural norms & traditions
- Religious beliefs
- Core values & general belief systems
- Accepted behaviour
- Coping with uncertainty
- Need for trust and safety
- The prioritization of individualism over the collective
- The prioritization of achievement over relationship
- Attitudes to time/deadlines, business processes, meetings and discussions

Figure 2: Executive Reflection: Embracing Rainbow Thinking

The practice of Executive Reflection can greatly enhance the way we move from our own ingrained habits and ways of being, into a broader more accepting mindset. If we are to survive and flourish in a global marketplace this will be vital to our success.

Our VUCA GVD World: *The Perfect Storm*

CHAPTER 3

Executive Reflection:
The Port in the Perfect Storm

Executive Reflection is the port in the storm – the oasis in the desert. It provides the maps, processes, support and resources to navigate today's VUCA GVD world from the inside out and outside in.

Following on from the definition of Executive Reflection given in Chapter 1, this chapter describes the modalities – the type and range of reflection and reflective practices – which can be developed and explored. There is no perfect way or one style fits all, but rather a range of processes which are offered and can be adapted and changed to suit the individual, team or business. The key here is appreciating that Executive Reflection's style of leadership is a way of being. It is a way of working with curiosity, inquiry, care, openness, courage and compassion. It shapes the next steps within a broader context of what is possible, needed and deliverable in the life cycle of a leader, team or business. This is fundamental because as Gardner and O'Brien remind us:

> Our state of being is the only real source of our ability to influence the world.[1]
>
> The quality of any intervention depends on the interior condition of the intervener.[2]

At its heart reflection is a simple (though not necessarily easy) flow of Retreat, Reflect and Return. Retreat is an intentional pausing to stop habitual thought and reaction. When we Reflect we immerse ourselves in not knowing, become aware of what is arising within us and around us, and notice what seeds of potential and possibility are wanting to emerge. When we Return we can use our discoveries to inform wise experimentation and action. While this contains an elegant simplicity, certain conditions and practices are essential for us to realize the full benefits of its creative and generative powers.

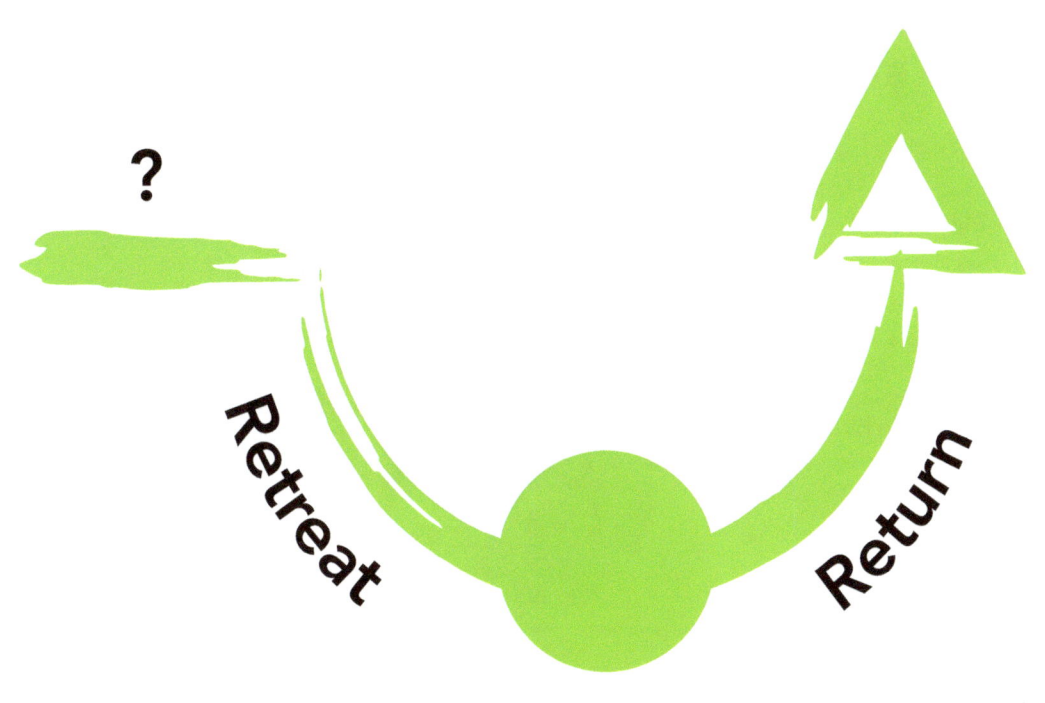

Putting in Place the Preconditions for Reflection

The preconditions for reflection are

i. making a commitment to working in this way

ii. working with a beginner's mindset

iii. creating a supportive environment for reflection, including finding the places, spaces, processes and people to support you

iv. paying attention to how you pay attention and developing your supportive mindfulness practices

v. remembering your own self-care is also needed as learning in this way can be challenging, daunting, frustrating, worrying yet also very rewarding and transformational.

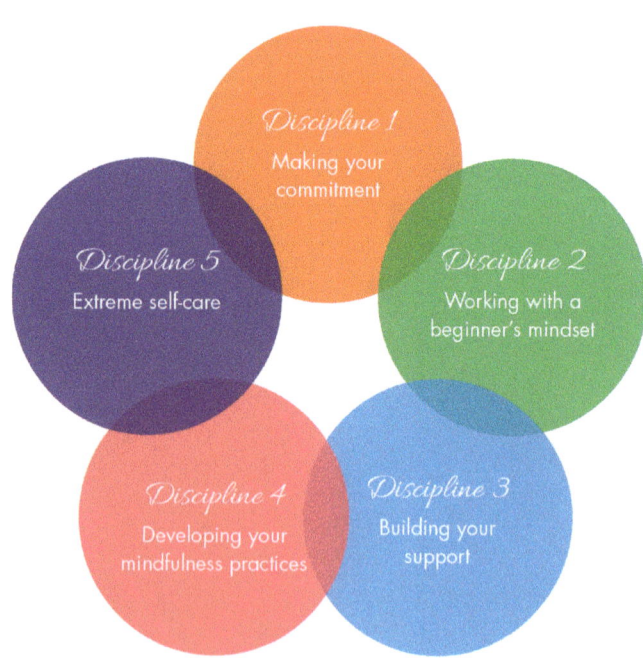

The rest of this chapter will focus on preparing for inquiry.

The Many Ways into Reflection

The good news is that there are many ways into reflection. Which method you use depends on what works best for you. The key is to get your reflective muscles working so that it becomes a natural way of working for you and your team. Expect difficulty and resistance at the start but, like skiing or surfing, you will soon find your flow.

Vignette

A director came to Executive Reflection as part of a national Leadership Development Programme she was participating in. The 1:1 sessions were an integral part of the programme. Initially reluctant, feeling that 'reflection is a luxury I cannot afford' the more she experienced the deep dive of the 1:1 sessions and the journaling and mindfulness practices she did in-between sessions, the more she saw her own need for reflection, concluding 'The more I do, the more I want to do.'

There are four types of reflection depending on the issue, context and timescale.[3] Criticality means the critical questioning and inquiry into underlying assumptions or patterns. In different combinations and at different times, all four are valuable and necessary.

1. **Spot Reflection** is reflection which can take place in the moment at a meeting, in the lift, over the water cooler, to check in, ground and centre.
2. **Reflection IN Action** is reflection which can take place as a meeting or a conversation is unfolding in real time, the better to shape what will happen next. For example, it might feel that a conversation is going round in circles, and pushing the pause button either privately or with the others in the room can help to gain perspective and see the deeper more systemic issues at play.
3. **Reflection ON Action** is reflection after an activity, event or incident has taken place to take the learning and apply it to future scenarios. For example this could be after a meeting which

has gone either well or badly. Time may be needed to extract the learning to achieve success again or do better next time.

4. **Reflection FOR Action** is reflection to be with the unknown, explore potential and possibility, and co-create with what is wanting to emerge from the field. For example this could be when new scenarios present, the path is unclear and innovation and creativity are needed.

Different Ways to Reflect

1. **Mindful Awareness**

   As Siegal writes:

   > Mindfulness is a form of mental activity that trains the mind to become aware of awareness itself and to pay attention to one's intention.[4]

   The good news is that mindfulness is available to us at any time. It can be a simple as focusing on the breath, grounding and centring. It works because it is a calming of our nervous system to return us to our natural curiosity, inquiry, openness and creativity. This opens us up to new ways of seeing, relating and thinking. Our capacity for Mindfulness can be developed through practice and via any hobby or activity which interrupts everyday habitual thoughts. Mindful activities may include reading, cookery, gardening, art, crafts, music, exercise, photography, massage and martial arts! The key is finding what works for you.

2. **Journaling**

   As Didion wrote:

   > I write entirely to find out what I am thinking, what I am looking at, what I see, and what it means, what I want and what I fear.[5]

   A regular journaling practice is arguably one of the most powerful tools to reflect. Free-flow writing – without worrying about spelling, punctuation or presentation – can help us to discharge negative emotions, celebrate what has gone well, process our experiences, see different perspectives, and create solutions to problems.

3. **Reading, Research and Learning from Others**

   Consciously stepping out and away from our own world can be a powerful stimulation and challenge to our habitual ways of seeing and thinking. Staying current and up to date is vital for innovation and creativity in the workplace, as is having new experiences in different contexts, which will stretch and challenge us and help us to grow. Companies like Apple and Google appreciate the value of this. They offer time out schemes for their staff so that they return refreshed and renewed. Research has also shown the value of having leaders role model the power of reflection through their stories.[6] This needs to permeate through to every level of the organization.

4. **Frameworks for Questioning**

   Reflection needs frameworks for questioning. It always starts with a question or wondering about something. Finding out what works – or which combinations work – for you and your workplace is the key here.

   American Military Review

   The American Military After Action Review (AAR) process is famous – but there are many others. An AAR is a professional discussion of an event, focused on performance standards, that enables soldiers to discover for themselves What happened, Why it happened and How to sustain strengths and improve on weaknesses.

   Retreat, Reflect, Return

   Here is another based on Retreat, Reflect and Return which is a simplified version of Scharmer's Theory U[7] and Patterson's 'Reflect to *Create!*'[7]

Retreat

i. What is my inquiry?
ii. What is inviting me to stop?
iii. What is my current reality?
iv. What am I assuming and what assumptions do I need to let go of to see afresh?

Reflect

v. What am I sensing to the Retreat section
vi. What am I sensing from my body and from the wider field?
vii. Am I being fully present to what wants to emerge?
viii. What new perspectives and possibilities are emerging?

Return

ix. What new choices for decision-making and elegant action are now emerging?

5. **Clean Language**

   Another helpful framework is Clean Language Methodology.

   This is at the forefront of cross-cultural working and building strong international relationships and enhances the effectiveness of innovative Executive Reflective Practice.[8]

   Clean Language was devised by psychotherapist David Grove. As far as possible, he wanted to find a way to keep his assumptions out of interactions with his clients, so he could work directly with their perceptions. It consists of thirty or so questions, asked in a measured and neutral way.

   David Grove spent time watching other practitioners at work and analyzing transcripts of them working with clients. He realized that they were subtly rewording what their clients were saying and felt this was robbing clients of some of their experience. He decided to keep his clients' words intact – by repeating them verbatim. He also considered what questions he could ask that would contain fewer presuppositions, while still directing attention to aspects of their experience that seemed to merit exploration. This is highly effective when working cross-culturally as it helps to remove subjective assumptions and unconscious bias.

   For example asking someone 'What are you thinking?' presupposes that a person is thinking something, and limits their possible responses. David 'cleaned' the question to become: 'Is there anything else about x?'

   - A statement like 'I want you to tell me how you feel about x' shifts a person's attention back and forth (I – you – me – you – x), so David also removed all pronouns, unless they were part of what the person was talking about. 'Tell me more' also turned into 'Is there anything else?'
   - He wanted to be specific about where he was directing a person's attention, so he introduced the word 'that' into many of his questions: 'What kind of x is that x?'
   - Since a person's experience is happening now (even if they're recalling a memory), he framed all questions in the present tense.
   - He wanted people to stay in their experience so he joined his questions into what they were saying by prefacing them with the word 'and' (see examples below). This enables the client to stay in the flow of the exchange and not be interrupted.

Clean Language is very flexible, ideal for Executive Reflection and is now used in many contexts:

- As a business development mode
- As a highly effective cross-cultural communication method
- As an interviewing method (it is used by the Metropolitan Police)
- As a way to model different skills and perceptions
- As a reflective practice methodology
- In business meetings
- For team building & engagement

(Adapted from 'Coaching Skills for Leaders in the Workplace' Jackie Arnold and with permission of James Lawley and Penny Tomkins.)[9]

The use of Clean Language adds great value when building strong international relationships as it is a respectful and highly effective communication technique bringing clarity to every exchange. It avoids assumptions and because it uses the language and mind view of every individual, it is highly effective. It enhances the sense of being heard and culturally respected, as clean language works with individuals at their pace and with their style of learning.

Clean Language techniques are aligned closely with modern 'enabling' principles of empathy and understanding, as opposed to traditional 'manipulative' (conscious or unconscious) methods of influence and persuasion and the projection of self-interest. Clean Language helps people to convey their own meaning, free of emotional or other distracting interpretation from others. As such Clean Language promotes better clarity of communications, neutrality and objectivity (absence of emotional 'spin', bias and prejudice), ease of understanding, and cooperative productive cross-cultural relationships.

This methodology also encourages being 'in the moment', allowing leaders the reflective space to understand what is going on right now for them and their teams. It focuses attention and leads to clarity when making decisions, planning and devising successful business strategies. It encourages honest self-reflection, quiet mind-body exploration and deeper understanding of complex situations – particularly in a Global Virtual and Diverse world.

6. **Group, Team or Peer Reflection**

   Setting up processes for review and reflection away from the busyness of doing is always good practice. Taking stock, sorting, clarifying, re-shaping and re-designing to navigate the present and co-create the future are key to discovering collective wisdom, securing both individual and collective engagement, and achieving high performance.

   Different formats can be used. The most powerful format can be easily adapted for any context and is a version of Nancy Kline's 'Time to Think'.[10] It is practiced as follows:

   - The Presenter raises their question or issue.
   - The Host asks any clarifying questions to hone the question for the group to work on.
   - The Presenter quietly listens as the group explores their issue.
   - The Host then invites each person in the group to have the Talking Stick. In turn each person offers – without giving criticism, advice or judgment – what they are noticing in themselves, what they are curious about, or what they are wondering about from the Practitioner's presentation. Everyone listens to the holder of the Talking Stick without interruption or discussion.
   - Three rounds are then suggested where group members start to build on each other's offers.
   - The Host then invites the Presenter to consider all that has been offered.
   - It is also OK for them to say that nothing has been useful. No discussion with the group is entered into.
   - The Host then offers any last comments which may be helpful.
   - The Host then invites each member of the group to reflect on their learning from working on the Presenter's issue, which they may want to apply to their life or work.

There are numerous other tools and creative processes to support the questioning and inquiry process. These include 360s, NLP, the Magic Box, Ladder of Inference, Transactional Analysis, Metaphor Cards, Labyrinths, Reflective Walking and World Cafés.

7. **Executive Reflection**

    Our research found that 1:1 Executive Reflection between a leader and a skilled practitioner is a very powerful and cost-effective way to become a reflective leader.[11]

    1:1 Executive Reflection is a hybrid practice which blends the best from the coaching, mentoring, supervision and adult learning and development fields to give leaders the personalized, tailor-made support, resourcing and inspiration to both work through live executive issues, and attend to their personal and professional development.

    1:1 Executive Reflection is defined as:

    > 1:1 Executive Reflection is an independently co-created learning partnership and distinct developmental practice built on trust, safety and service. Executive Reflection provides a uniquely creative, compassionate, resourceful and generative oasis for leaders to gain a robust and deep awareness and super-vision of WHO they are, WHY they lead and HOW they lead. The process attends to both their personal and professional development that in turn resources leaders to lead wisely in turbulent times.

    Executive Reflection Practitioners are seasoned and skilled practitioners. As we established in our research:

    > The Practitioner works as an independent and confidential witness, companion, mirror and observer providing a creative space and non judgmental container for deep thinking and reflection. The Practitioner creates the personal and environmental field conditions for the leader to gain profound insight, resourcing and learning to ignite personal, team and organizational change and wise action. The Practitioner enables and supports the leader to step into the new leadership style of Executive Reflection.

As Karyn Prentice from Prentice Fletcher Associates and one of the research participants wrote:

> In a world rushing at speed it can seem counter-intuitive to do the opposite and go slower. Because I believe that pushing the pause button is a singular act of sanity, and an aspect of ethical maturity for leaders and for us all, I was delighted to have the opportunity to be a part of this project. Finding ways to navigate the often sticky territory of our thinking and all the multiple layers of the demands reminds me of the words of a noted comedian who said that 'the workings of her mind were so complex it was like a really provocative neighbourhood one should never visit alone'.
>
> The partnership of Executive Reflection challenges both parties to be willing to walk through that gateway and explore fresh and creative thinking. Having been paired with a global leader we had conversations that opened paths around their current thinking in a space that was not like any other. It was not coaching, not consultancy, but a mental meeting place that was like the rose on a compass. It can't tell you where to go but it can be a place to take a reading of all the information and see afresh.
>
> I was surprised, delighted and excited about how we found a way to go deep to the heart of the questions that were most urgent and to reflect together on the current issues of the moment. In a hybrid mix of practices in relatively short time, we refined our learning partnership. I learned by stretching into new territory and landscape and my client explored where all the roads in the neighbourhood met. I believe we connected and reconnected to the heart of the matter in each session as key concerns were reframed, values and needs realigned and the compass re-set for the future.

6. Retreats

Residential retreats in beautiful surroundings give leaders an accelerated and immersive experience to embrace, practice, embed and embody this new leadership style.

Retreats are especially powerful when combined with a programme of 1:1 Executive Reflection support both before and after the retreat. This enables the individual to focus on the elements and behaviours needed for specific situations and cultures.

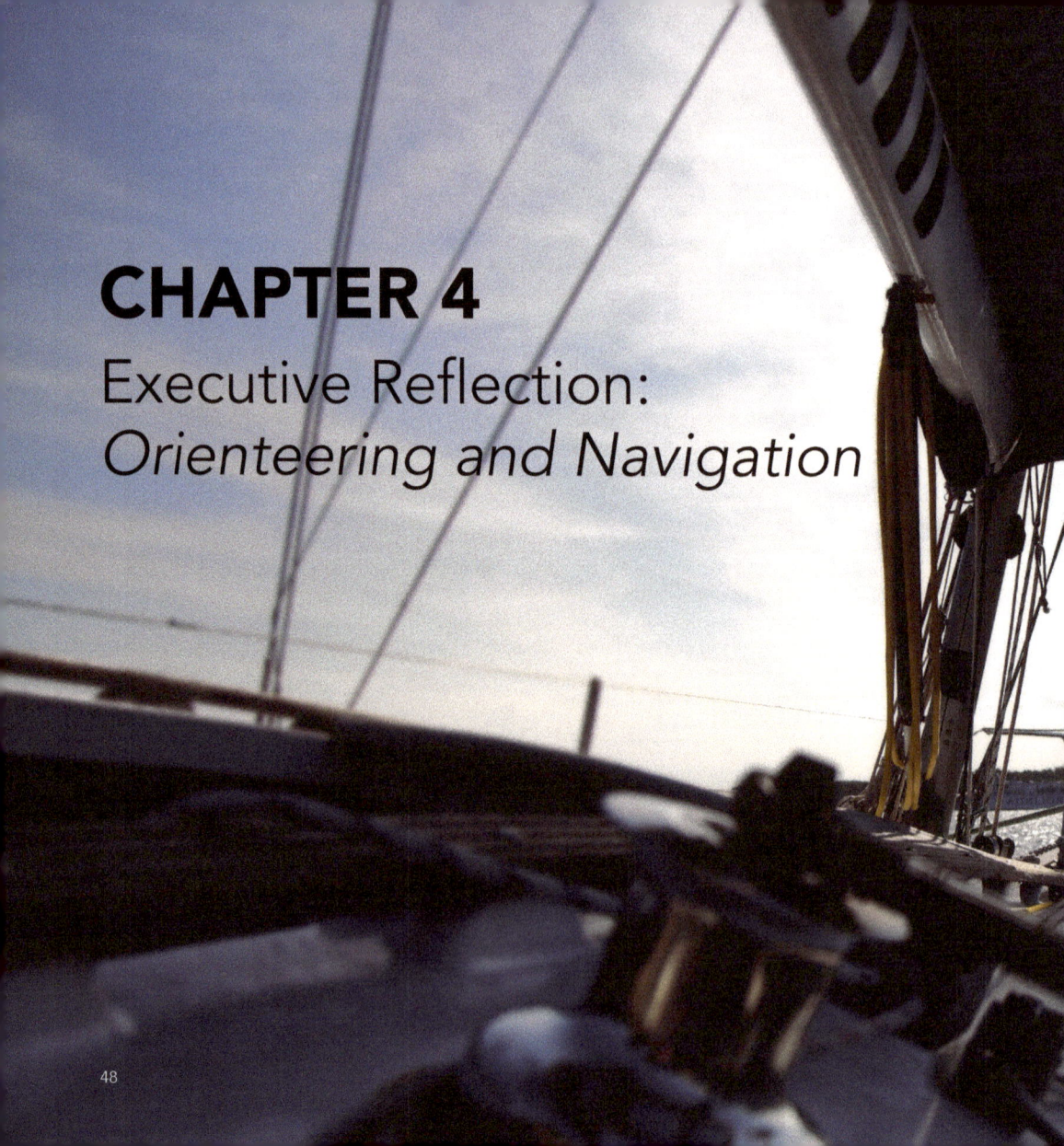

CHAPTER 4
Executive Reflection: *Orienteering and Navigation*

Figure 3: Reflection As Navigation

Executive Reflection can help leaders to navigate today's perfect storm to set a course and find direction. Executive Reflection helps leaders to work wisely with courage, compassion, intelligence and skill.

Our research and our experience has shown us that Executive Reflection can offer leaders the following opportunities:

1. **To Reflect**

    Executive Reflection gives leaders the opportunity to inquire into and develop their own leadership style. It enables them to bring their best selves to their work and build teams around them in order to complement the skills, capacities and competencies needed to deliver. Executive Reflection gives leaders the opportunity to hold a mirror to themselves, to see themselves as others see them and observe the impact this has. With it they may learn to understand their own triggers, gifts and blind spots, to challenge their own assumptions and mindsets, and to finesse their relational and communication capacities for leading in a VUCA GVD world.

Executive Reflection helps leaders to become comfortable working with radical uncertainty in order to find new paths. Executive Reflection gives leaders the opportunity to look into both who they are being and who they are becoming as they work, and to notice how this emerges in their leadership style and impact.

> As one leader reported during our research: 'Reflection provides a space away from the busyness of business so that the leader can slow down, reflect, connect with what is important to them, gain fresh and useful insights, learn about and lean into their strengths, explore and better understand complex situations and discover new and more effective ways of approaching challenges and opportunities.' Another said, 'I owe it [reflection] to myself. Reflection is foundational and fundamental to me living and working deliberately.'

2. **To Reconnect**

    Executive Reflection gives leaders the opportunity to connect and reconnect with themselves, with their teams, and with the purpose of their organization. It allows them to pay careful attention to the webs of relationship, connection and communication which keep the organization moving, living and breathing. It also ensures that the organization's purpose, intention, mission and values are aligned with its actual behaviours and actions, and the felt experience of team members, clients and stakeholders.

    > 'My work means I get so twisted out of shape I lose who I am. Reflection reminds me who I am and why I do what I do and how I can do it better. Reflection brings me home to myself.' Another said, 'I love finding the links between things! ... I love finding the "aha" moment – it is a bit like a dopamine hit!'

3. **To Relate**

    Executive Reflection gives leaders the opportunity to inquire into the quality of their relationships. Leadership is a relational act, working in and through the relationships which leaders are able to create, design and maintain.

    > 'Reflection gives me the opportunity to heighten my self-awareness and that can only help you as a leader because this makes you connect better to people by being more aware of yourself and how to engage with people ... how you are as a person and how you engage with people.'

4. **To Re-language**

   Executive Reflection helps leaders to find new ways of using language to help others to connect and relate to each other. It helps to establish what is needed.

   Idioms, metaphors, definitions, sentence construction and interpretation greatly vary within the same culture and between cultures. Meaning can get lost in translation with unintended consequences. Executive Reflection helps leaders to understand the impact of miscuing, as well as finding new forms of expression which work.

   > 'Reflection,' said one leader, 'helped me to understand my impact on others. I remember this one occasion when I was really busy, rushing, missing subtle cues – and not so subtle cues! – that I was imposing my agenda on the team … that I was not listening to them …. and they became passive aggressive with me. The project was almost derailed because of my insensitivity. And this was the wake-up call I needed.'

   > Another said, 'I am now able to step into another's shoes much easier, see what is going on for the other person and hear at all levels.'

5. **To Remember**

   Executive Reflection gives leaders the opportunity to remember why they lead and who they want to be when they lead. In the busyness of life and work it is all too easy to forget ourselves, to lose sight of our own core values, purpose and intention, and to forget our own direction. Executive Reflection helps leaders remember themselves in the busyness of business.

   > For one leader 'Reflection is the process of being able to bring one's mindful awareness to all of the leadership endeavour through a consideration of self in the context of the past, present and future.'

   > Another said, 'I really value the personal space to think, and carry me forward into the next phase.'

6. **To Review**

    Executive Reflection gives leaders the opportunity to pause and review; to look back to both understand the present and face forwards; to understand what is working and not working, why this is so and what might need to change.

    > 'Reflection is a safe space to voice out challenges and find one's way to step ahead … stepping back … embracing what is to move forward.'

7. **To Re-evaluate**

    Executive Reflection gives leaders the feedback needed to evaluate their course and direction and establish if it still makes sense. It also allows them to gather data and intelligence from a wide variety of sources in order to check accuracy, and the validity of the current approach. This is feedback for feeding forward.

    > 'Reflection,' says one global leader, 'is the discipline and the process that keeps me on track… evaluative feedback and feedforward is key … Is what we are doing working? What do our clients think and want? Is there a better way of doing things? Are we on course? What else is happening that we need to factor into our thinking? What is coming over the horizon?'

8. **To Reframe, Re-align and Re-Set**

    Executive Reflection gives leaders the opportunity to review with courage and then reframe, re-align, regroup or re-set themselves, their values, their teams and their organizations as needed.

    > 'Reflection, gives me the space and permission to take the learning – good or bad – and then to move on.'

9. **To Redesign and Reform**

   Executive Reflection gives leaders the courage to change – to co-create, to redesign, to reform and transform in order to stop what is no longer working, reshape the old or bring the new into life. Redesign or reform is the key to innovation and transformation where more of the same is no longer enough. Old assumptions, mindsets, or ways of working, relating or communicating need to be courageously relinquished for new potential and possibilities to emerge.

   > 'Reflection creates a spaciousness for something new to emerge – for something new to be evoked that was not there before. It creates an opportunity to see things from different perspectives and get a new sense of what is emerging and what is needed.'

   Another global leader said, 'Reflection has enabled me to work in an emergent future domain which has its presence now. I have become more exploratory, more freeform, which is helping me to work so much more creatively.'

10. **To Rest, Refresh and Recharge**

    Executive Reflection gives leaders a safe port in which to rest, refresh, refuel and recharge. Rest is key to wellbeing. Planned periods of rest and relaxation are necessary for all round health and wellbeing. Without them, leaders and their teams risk short termism, unacceptably high levels of stress or burnout, and loss of productivity. Executive Reflection can help leaders and their teams feel valued, seen and appreciated.

    > 'Work is a part of who I am and is not all of who I am. Reflection helps me to manage my life and my work within it.'

    Another said, 'I have to remember to give myself permission to stop and reflect … And there is something very wrong if we are unable to stop and pause.'

11. **To Resource**

    Executive Reflection helps leaders find the practical sources of help, advice and support they need to lead. Executive Reflection helps leaders to grow both personally and professionally. Executive Reflection also gives leaders a safe space to resource themselves for the long haul by attending to their own emotional, physical, psychological and spiritual wellbeing.

The case was made by Barrett Brown when he wrote how rich reflective learning environments enable people to develop the enhanced and highly attuned mental, emotional, and relational capacities that others don't have.[1]

> They not only see and feel situations and people differently, but they see and feel more than other leaders. They sense more connections, nuances, perspectives, and possibilities. They are able to act with greater wisdom and deeper care than ever before, and this empowers them to be able to reliably generate organizational transformation. It also strengthens their ability to effectively respond to the complex, ambiguous, and sophisticated challenges of 21st century leadership.'

> 'I do not think I could work at this pace, at this intensity, at this level of responsibility, with the challenges ahead of us without taking time out to reflect. I find that reflection helps me to resource myself – for me to pay attention to my own thoughts, feelings, hopes, intentions, passions and needs. Then I can make choices about what I need to do. Reflection helps me to feel calmer and more in control.'

Summary

The opportunities of Executive Reflection for leaders to reflect, to reconnect, to relate, to re-language, to remember, to review, to re-evaluate, to reframe, realign and reset, to redesign and reform, to rest, refresh and recharge and to resource is captured in the graphic opposite.

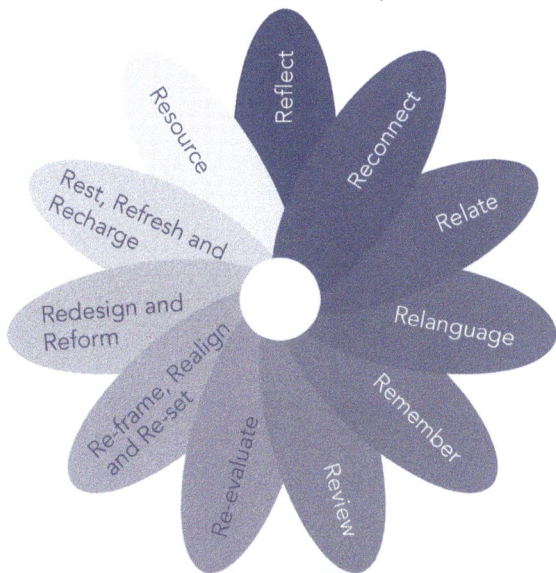

CALL TO ACTION

Our purpose is to build a new global cross-cultural leadership style called Executive Reflection. We believe Executive Reflection will support global leaders to meet the UN Global Goals for 2030.

We are a specialist group of cross-cultural, multi-lingual professionals from diverse backgrounds, cultures and experiences. We have all qualified as Executive Coaches and studied with the Coaching Supervision Academy or similar. Our values start with our own reflective practice and self-awareness. Reflective learning and practice is at the heart of all our programmes. We offer 1:1 programmes, Global Leadership Retreats, and online training programmes, resources and support. We create spaces and places where leaders can grow their awareness, while meeting with and learning from like-minded leaders from all over the world.

Visit our websites www.coaching4executives.com or www.elainepattersonexcutivecoaching.com for booking and further information.

More Background to the Project

Jackie Arnold and **Elaine Patterson** are both International Executive Coaches and Coaching Supervisors. Jackie's company – Coach4Executives – specializes in cross-cultural and intercultural leadership, communication and training. Elaine's company – The Centre for Reflection and Creativity – specializes in reflection, creativity and people development.

The great majority of CEOs expect that business complexity is going to increase and … more than half doubt their ability to manage it. The sheer difficulty of keeping a corporation afloat in such turbulent economic, political, and social water is beyond most leaders' experience and capacity.

Perhaps more importantly, in addition to our shared credentials we discovered that we had both lived abroad and worked globally with leaders across many different sectors and cultures. We coined the acronym GVD as the missing dimension to the already widely used acronym VUCA (Volatile, Uncertain, Complex and Ambiguous) GVD stands for Global, Virtual and Diverse.

We had both obtained – at different times – CSA's Diploma in Coaching Supervision and knew how it had transformed our own leadership and coaching and supervision practices, so we asked ourselves, What might happen if the coach supervisors who had been trained by the CSA could also extend their offer to leaders? We called this new practice '1:1 Executive Reflection' and took the latest research and the best from the fields of coaching, supervision, adult development and international work to support and resource leaders working in a VUCA GVD. With the help of our Research Supervisor Dr. Alison Hodge, we then decided to design a study to test our hypothesis. The title was:

An Action Research Inquiry to Explore the Relevance and Value of Executive Reflection to Leaders in a Global, Virtual and Diverse World.

We worked in partnership, pairing ten senior global Volunteer Leaders with ten senior global Volunteer Practitioners who had been trained by CSA Ltd. What we ultimately discovered was that the practice of 1:1 Executive Reflection was just one – albeit it critically important – component to supporting a new leadership style of Executive Reflection. This new style is where you the leader come to embrace and role model a very exciting and diverse body and range of reflective practices.

We believe these practices sit on the frontiers of adult learning and development with potential to accelerate the learning, creativity and innovation needed for you and your team or organization to both survive and thrive in today's VUCA GVD world.

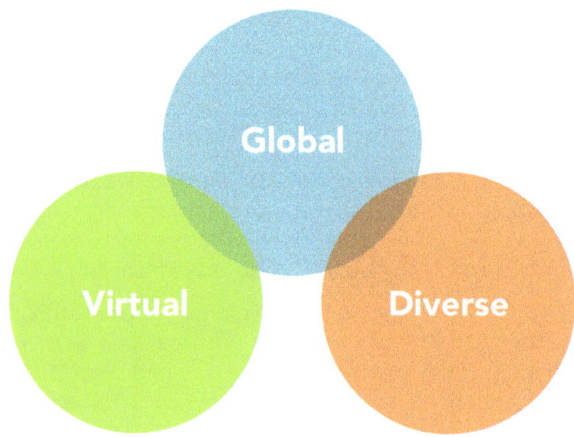

Visit our websites www.coaching4executives.com or www.elainepattersonexcutivecoaching.com for booking and further information.

REFERENCES

Glossary

[1] Johansen, B. (2012) Leaders Make the Future: Ten New Leadership Skills for an Uncertain World San Francisco Berrett-Koehler Publishers Inc.

Introduction

[1] Drucker, P. F. (1995) Managing in Times of Great Change. Abingdon, Oxon. Pp25 and cited in Hutchins, G. (2016) https://thenatureofbusiness.org/2014/05/28/a-new-logic-beyond-the-illusion-of-separation/

[2] Einstein, A. (1943) Quote cited in The Real Problem is in the Hearts of Men. New York Times Magazine 23rd June 1946. [Internet] http://icarus-falling.blogspot.co.uk/2009/06/einstein-enigma.html. [Downloaded 25th May 2016]

[3] Scharmer, O. (2018) The Essentials of Theory U – Core Principles and Applications California, Berrett-Koehler Publishers Inc.

[4] Bushlong, J. O. (2013) Belonging Everywhere and Nowhere: Insights into Counselling the Globally Mobile. Indiania, Mango Tree Publications

[5] https://www.globalgoals.org/

[6] Downloaded 2st November 2018 from https://businesslinkedteams.com/system/files/white-papers/Grow%20Your%20Own%20Leader_0.pdf Business Linked Teams commissioned independent research company Vitreous World to conduct research into how senior HR professionals manage internal leadership development strategies and programmes. The research company surveyed a sample of 100 HR decision makers in the UK with 250+ employees. The interviews were conducted in the Summer of 2018

[7] IBM (2010) Capitalizing on Complexity: Insights from the Global Chief Executive Office Study. Available at http://public.dhe.ibm.com/common/ssi/ecm/en/gbe03297u-sen.GBE03297USEN.PDF [Accessed 15th December 2013]

Chapter 1: Executive Reflection: A New and Distinct Leadership Style

[1] Owen, H. Ed. (2000) *In Search of Leaders*. Chichester, John Wiley & Sons Ltd

[2] 'Who You Are is How You Coach' was coined by the Coaching Supervision Academy. The concept is further explored in Patterson, E. (2019) *Reflect to Create! The Dance of Reflection for Creative Leadership, Professional Practice and Supervision*. Pp5. London, Centre for Reflection and Creativity Ltd.

[3] Siegal, D. (2015) *The Developing Mind – How Relationships and the Brain Interact to Shape Who we Are*. New York, Guildford Press.

[4] Lewis, T., Amini, F. & Lannon, R. (2001) *A General Theory of Love*. New York, Random House

[5] Kolb D. (1984). *Experiential Learning: Experience as the Source of Learning and Development*. Englewood Cliffs, New Jersey: Prentice Hall

[6] Patterson, E. (2015) *'What are Leaders' Experiences of Reflection?' What leaders and leadership developers need to know from the findings of an exploratory research study*. Reflective Practice, Volume 16 Number 5, pp 636–51 [Internet] http://dx.doi.org/10.1080/14623943.2015.1064386

Chapter 2: Our VUCA GVD World: The Perfect Storm

[1] For more information see DISC Profiling at www.discprofile.com; FIRO B at www.cpp.com; Hogan Personality Inventory at www.hoganassessments.com; or Myers Briggs Foundation at www.myersbriggs.org

Chapter 3: Executive Reflection: The Port in the Perfect Storm

[1] Gardner, H. (2006) *Frames of Mind*. MA, Perseus Books

[2] Sharmer, O. (2014) *Collective Mindfulness: The Leaders New Work*. Available from: www.huffingtonpost.com/otto-scharmer/collective-mindfulness. [Accessed 6th February 2014]

[3] Schon, D. (1983) *The Reflective Practitioner: How Professionals Think In Action*. US, Basic Books Ltd.

[4] Downloaded 17th June 2017 from http://goodreads.com/author/quotes/191925 Daniel.J.Siegel

[5] Downloaded 20th March 2017 from https://www.goodreads.com/quotes/22534

[6] Patterson, E. (2015) 'What are Leaders' Experiences of Reflection?' What leaders and leadership

developers need to know from the findings of an exploratory research study, Reflective Practice, Volume 16 Number 5, pp 636–51 [Internet] http://dx.doi.org/10.1080/14623943.2015.1064386

[7] Scharmer, O. (2018) *The Essentials of Theory U – Core Principles and Applications.* California, Berrett-Koehler Publishers Inc.

[8] Lawley, J Tomkins, P. (2013) *Metaphors in Mind Transformation Through Symbolic Modelling.* London, The Developing Company Press

[9] Patterson, E. (2019) *Reflect to Create! The Dance of Reflection for Creative Leadership, Professional Practice and Supervision.* London, Centre for Reflection and Creativity Ltd.

[10] Kline, N. (1999) *Time to Think: Listening to Ignite the Human Mind.* London, Ward Lock

[11] 2019 https://www.theparliamentaryreview.co.uk/organizations /coach-4-executives

Chapter 4: Executive Reflections' Orientation and Way Finding

[1] Brown, B.C. (2013) *The Future of Leadership for Conscious Capitalism.* MetaIntegral Associates. Available from: www. https://associates.metaintegral.org/.../future-leadership-conscious-capitalism. [Accessed 15th December 2013]

References

www.ingramcontent.com/pod-product-compliance
Lightning Source LLC
Chambersburg PA
CBHW051254110526
44588CB00026B/2990